How to Teach the Bible so that People Meet God

Andrew Page

VTR
Publications

ISBN 978-3-95776-035-7

Cover design: Chris Allcock
Printed by Lightning Source

Contents

Acknowledgements

I thank God for all those in various countries to whom I have taught this material in workshops.

I am grateful to Chris Allcock for the cover design and especially to Thomas Mayer for his vision in publishing this book.

I thank James Musson, Biddy Taylor, Nick Berryman and Luke Avery for their comments and encouragement about the completed manuscript.

This book is dedicated to everyone who longs to see the Holy Spirit using the Bible more and more so that people meet God. I pray that he will use this material to equip many Bible teachers. To God be the glory!

Andrew Page
www.howtoteachthebible.org

Introduction

How to Teach the Bible

The Bible is the word of God. If Christians and churches neglect the word of God, they will not grow and they will not enjoy the relationship they have come into with Jesus.

Here are some basic questions which are designed to get us thinking about the importance of teaching the Bible. My answers are intended to convince you that this book is worth reading.

And working through.

1. Why is Bible teaching sometimes difficult?

I can think of a number of reasons.

a. Teaching the Bible is a spiritual battle

If you read the Gospels you will see how often the powers of evil interrupted Jesus as he was teaching the word of God.

The apostle Paul experienced the same thing.

So it is inevitable that we too will sometimes find that preparing or giving a Bible talk is a real struggle.

b. Some Bible passages are harder than others to preach

If it is a part of the Bible you have not studied before, then of course you will find that more difficult.

And most Bible teachers will find it more of a challenge to teach a passage from Revelation than a passage from Mark's Gospel.

c. Some Christians with the gift of teaching have never had any training

The Holy Spirit may have given you this particular spiritual gift, but that does not mean that you are automatically a great Bible teacher.

We need training.

So if you find Bible teaching difficult that does not necessarily mean that you do not have the gift. It may simply be that no one has given you some basic help.

And that is what this book is aiming to do.

d. Most Christians do not have the gift of teaching

If you are a Christian to whom the Holy Spirit has given other gifts and not this one, then inevitably you will find teaching the Bible difficult.

And it means you should be serving God in other areas, in ways that fit with the gifts he *has* given you.

If you would like to find out if you have the gift of teaching, this book is a good place to start.

2. So why did I write this book?

My belief is that if we are gifted at something we find it easy. For example, ask an Olympic cyclist if she finds cycling difficult.

She will doubtless reply that the training is sometimes incredibly hard or that the disappointments can be crippling. But she will laugh at the thought that she might find cycling, as such, difficult.

It's the same with teaching the Bible. If the Holy Spirit has given you the spiritual gift of teaching, of course struggles and hard work will be in store for you. But teaching the Bible will not be difficult.

The first reason I have written this book is to provide a basic how-to guide for Christians who are getting opportunities to teach the Bible to others.

The second reason is this: I think there is a mystique in parts of the Church about Bible teaching, so that preachers are even seen as being closer to God than the rest of us.

It's not true. Bible teaching is incredibly important for the Church – it can be a supernatural event. But Bible teachers are not closer to God than anyone else.

And the third reason? I am convinced that Bible teaching that takes the Bible seriously and is open to the Holy Spirit makes it more likely that people will have an encounter with God.

3. What is the difference between preaching and teaching?

Christians give different answers to this question; I am not claiming that mine is the only correct one.

Some say that teaching is communicating Bible content, while preaching is doing it with fire and with application.

But I don't think this distinction is biblical.

If you look at the lists of spiritual gifts in the New Testament, you will not find two gifts (preaching and teaching) but one: teaching (see Romans 12:7, 1 Corinthians 12:28, Ephesians 4:11 and 1 Peter 4:11).

So in this book I use the terms preaching and Bible teaching interchangeably.

I don't mind if you disagree with me; the important thing is that you know how I am using the words.

4. So what do I mean by preaching / Bible teaching?

I realise that there are various ways to teach the Bible. But in this book I focus on one particular kind of preaching: the teaching of a Bible passage.

Of course there is a place for topic preaching. Here, the speaker announces the topic – prayer, for example. Then, using a number of different verses and passages from around the Bible, they talk about prayer.

The danger with this approach is that the listeners admire the ability and the agility of the preacher.

In my opinion the teaching of one Bible passage is much more powerful, especially if the listeners have the text in front of them, either in a Bible or projected on to a screen.

Please do not misunderstand me. I am not ruling out topic teaching. I am just saying that there is a special power in the teaching of a Bible passage.

I have written this book because there are many churches in which this approach to Bible teaching is hardly ever practised and because I long for the Bible to be taught more and more in this way.

5. So who is this book for?

How to Teach the Bible so that People Meet God has been written for three groups of people.

First, it is for Christians who want to find out if they have the gift of teaching.

Second, it is for Christians with the gift of teaching who want to grow in their use of the gift.

And, third, it is for Christians with the gift of teaching who want to train others to teach the Bible.

If you come into any of those three categories, this book is for you.

6. How should this book be used?

a. Individually or with others

How to Teach the Bible so that People Meet God is designed as a practical course – it is unashamedly a how-to book.

You may want to work through it on your own. Or you might decide to do this with a friend. This friend may be at the same stage as you, as far as preaching is concerned, or they may be a much more experienced Bible teacher than you are.

So you decide.

But I want to encourage you to consider meeting up regularly with at least one other Christian as you work through this book.

b. Not just reading but also doing the homework

That word 'homework' may have put you off already!

But it is important. If you just read this book it will be of little benefit to you. When we want to develop a skill, we need to practise.

If you flick through the book you will see white boxes and grey boxes. The white boxes are simply for reading, but the grey boxes are headed up 'Something to do'.

I hope you will take time to work on the suggestions in the grey boxes – either alone or with others.

Let me prove to you how seriously I take this.

If you do decide to do the homework, you will want to see my own suggestions and answers. But I have deliberately not put these in an appendix.

If I were reading a book like this and the author's suggestions were in an appendix, I would probably not bother doing the homework; instead I would just turn to the back of the book.

I hope that putting my answers and suggestions on www.howtoteachthe bible.org will make it less likely that you will go for the lazy option!

c. With lots of prayer

The danger with a how-to book about Bible teaching is that you read it and think: "I can do this now – I've worked through the book!"

This brings us back to the issue of spiritual battle.

Unless we are trusting in the power of the Holy Spirit and asking God to equip us and change us, there is no point in reading the book at all.

I am praying that God will be at work in you as you ask him to equip you to teach the Bible so that people meet God.

I hope you will continue to read.

My belief is that the following ingredients are essential if we are to grow as Bible teachers: a model, a method and a mentor.

We will examine these ingredients in the three main parts of the book.

Enjoy!

Part One

A Model

We need to find a model.

Most learning doesn't happen in a vacuum. The best learning comes from watching someone doing something they are good at – and then copying them. So I remember as a sixteen-year-old watching my father wallpapering a room and then trying it myself. And it worked.

This is a biblical principle. Paul tells the Christians in Corinth "Follow my example, as I follow the example of Christ" (1 Cor 11:1). And there was something similar happening with Jesus and his Father during the three years of his public ministry: "Very truly I tell you, the Son can do nothing by himself; he can do only what he sees his Father doing, because whatever the Father does the Son also does" (Jn 5:19).

1. Our need

So, when it comes to preaching, we need to find a model. Doubtless you can think of one or two Bible teachers who are examples for you in different ways.

But don't look for a model who wears nice shirts; or whose jokes you like; or who constantly comes up with new explanations for Bible passages which no one else has thought of in 2,000 years of church history.

Instead, look for someone who loves God, who handles the Bible responsibly and enthusiastically, and through whose preaching people encounter God.

You may want to read that last paragraph again. Does anyone spring to mind?

2. My experience

My own models for preaching, especially when I was starting out, were John Stott and David Jackman.

I first heard John Stott preach when I was a student. During his decades of Bible teaching at All Souls Church, Langham Place in London, he spoke at countless conferences. When I first heard John Stott preach I had two reactions. First, I thought "This isn't clever – everything he's saying is in the Bible passage we're looking at." And second I thought "But why have I never noticed that in this passage before?" The Holy Spirit was making the Bible alive to me; I was encountering God.

So I was soon grabbing every opportunity to hear John Stott preach – and to read his books of Bible teaching too.

My second model for preaching has been David Jackman. When David became the minister of Above Bar Church, Southampton, I was his assistant for a little over three years. I suppose that during that time I heard more than 200 David Jackman sermons, and I was struck by his great faithfulness to the Bible and his quite extraordinary clarity in explaining and applying it. I was experiencing Bible teaching as a supernatural event.

This is where I made a mistake. I tried to become a second David Jackman. And, astonishingly, it didn't work!

I think it took about a year before the Lord got it into my head that if he had wanted two David Jackmans he would have made two David Jackmans. But in his wisdom and humour he had created one David Jackman (that was his wisdom) and one Andrew Page (that was his humour).

This doesn't mean that I threw overboard everything I had learnt from listening to David preach. Instead I started asking myself the question "What have I learnt from David which I must never let go of?" – and then putting those things into practice using *my* style and *my* personality. And it worked. God was using David's example to teach me to teach the Bible.

3. Your search

If you cannot think of a model Bible teacher it is time to pray and ask God for his help. Ask some friends for advice as to which books to read and where to go online. But don't choose a model just because others are enthusiastic – it must be someone whose Bible teaching God is using in your own life.

But I suspect that most of you who are reading this don't have to look for a model Bible teacher. You are already thinking of someone – someone God uses to make the Bible come alive to you in such a way that a supernatural event takes place.

Sometimes you will describe this experience as the Holy Spirit speaking God's word into your heart. Sometimes it will be being filled with joy as you realise that your Maker is communicating with you personally through his word. Sometimes it will be the Holy Spirit using the Bible to make you aware of your sin and to call you to turn from evil and follow Jesus fully. And sometimes it will be an amazement at the death and resurrection of Jesus, resulting in a new determination to worship him and live for his glory.

But always it will be an encounter with God.

Something to do (1)

1. If nobody springs to mind who is a model preacher for you, ask God to bring you into contact with someone who can be a model for you as you teach the Bible.

2. But if you can think of one or two Bible teacher models, thank God for them. And thank God for what he has done in your life through them.

3. What do you particularly appreciate about the way they teach the Bible? Ask God to build those qualities into your life – and into your Bible teaching.

Part Two

A Method

Some books about Bible teaching resist teaching a method. Instead they confine themselves to passing on basic principles: make sure you are faithful to the Bible passage, it is important to be clear, application matters immensely.

But for most of us this isn't enough.

Suppose you cannot swim and you have decided to ask me to teach you. I *could* decide to teach you basic principles: don't breathe under water, wave your arms and legs around, stay away from the deep end.

But that won't get you very far. What needs to happen is that I teach you a method of swimming, by which I mean a number of steps you can follow. Now of course, once you have started swimming you may find that you are going to do some things differently from the way I taught them to you in my method. That is fine. But a method is essential if you want to get started.

It is the same with preaching.

But there is something else that needs saying here. Those books on preaching which do teach a method are often rather complicated: I once saw one book (which was excellent in many ways) which offered me 38 steps on the way to preparing a sermon.

The very thought makes my brain shut down.

A method is not only essential, it must also be simple. Think of swimming again. Once you have learnt to swim there are lots of refinements and techniques you can incorporate into your style. But put those refinements and techniques into the basic method and you freak people out. The basic method needs to be just that: basic.

It is the same with preaching.

So the method I am teaching in this book consists of three steps. If you are looking for material about the different way parables should be preached from narrative or poetry, you will not find it here. This is partly because I want to make this method simple.

But there is another reason too.

My impression is that most people who have received the spiritual gift of teaching know instinctively that you don't preach a parable the same way as a miracle story: the Holy Spirit who has given them the gift helps them to see how it needs to be used differently with different parts of the Bible.

Of course all of us have blind spots. But if a Bible teacher preaches a parable as if it were an extract from Paul's Letter to the Colossians, a good friend can help them out, either by explaining the issue or by pointing them to a chapter on the subject in a book about preaching. That is why Part Three of this book is going to be so important.

So a method is essential and it must be simple. I hope you will try these three steps for yourself.

Step One: Study the passage in context

This is where we must start. It is obvious but so important that it is worth spelling out: if we are going to teach a Bible passage we have to find out what that passage means.

When I was living in Austria as a mission partner sent out by my home church, I was invited by a church to preach one Sunday. They had recently started a sermon series in the Letter to the Hebrews and the passage they gave me was Hebrews 3:1-6 – not something I would ever have chosen for myself.

Four questions help me to study a Bible passage. I am going to show you how I used them to study Hebrews 3:1-6, and then ask you to try the same thing with another passage. But let me first stress that as I study I am asking the Holy Spirit to give me wisdom and insight.

1 Therefore, holy brothers and sisters, who share in the heavenly calling, fix your thoughts on Jesus, the apostle and high priest whom we confess.
2 He was faithful to the one who appointed him, just as Moses was faithful in all God's house.
3 Jesus has been found worthy of greater honour than Moses, just as the builder of a house has greater honour than the house itself.
4 For every house is built by someone, but God is the builder of everything.
5 Moses was faithful as a servant in all God's house, testifying to what would be said in the future.
6 But Christ is faithful as a Son over God's house. And we are his house, if we hold on to our courage and the hope of which we boast.

Hebrews 3:1-6

Q1. What was the original meaning?

a. Why did the writer write this book?

If you write me an email I can find out why you sent it by simply reading it through. So I am not going to grab a commentary or a Bible dictionary. I will read through the whole of Hebrews. And then it becomes clear: the first readers were Jewish Christians who were being persecuted; under pressure, the temptation was to let go of Jesus and their Christian faith and slip back into Judaism.

Of course one reason the writer wrote this book is that the Holy Spirit inspired him to. But the human authors of Scripture were not machines: at the same time as the Spirit was moving them to write, they knew *why* they were writing.

Quite often there is something near the beginning or the end of a Bible book which tells us why the writer has written it. The clues in Hebrews are there at the beginning *and* at the end. Very early on there is a warning not to drift away from the faith (2:1-3) and the first verses of chapter 1 suggest that it was essential the readers realised just how wonderful Jesus was (1:1-3). So it is not difficult to work out why this 'word of exhortation' (13:22) was so important.

This discovery, which I might confirm by looking at a commentary, means that I will be looking at Hebrews 3:1-6 in context. If we ignore the context we will never find the real meaning.

> An archbishop was about to embark on a speaking tour of the USA. His friends advised him to be very careful at press conferences, because journalists would try to trap him with trick questions. On arrival in the States he experienced his first press conference. The first journalist asked if he would be visiting any nightclubs while he was in New York. The archbishop realised he must be very careful. So he smiled and said *'Are* there any nightclubs in New York?' The next day the headlines read: 'Archbishop's first question: Are there any nightclubs in New York?'

That story shows how important context is.

b. Why did the writer write these verses?

In other words, how do they fit in to the whole book?

With Hebrews 3:1-6 this is fairly straightforward. The writer is comparing various aspects of the Jewish religion with Jesus and the Christian Gospel. So in chapter 3 he comes to Moses, one of the greatest heroes of the Jewish faith; verses 1-6 are basically a comparision between Moses and Jesus.

c. What do the individual words mean?

At this stage it is important to ask lots of questions. And we need to be clear that we will not find the answers in an English dictionary. The cliché is true: Bible words have Bible meanings.

And remember that one author may use a word differently from the way another author uses it.

So I start at Hebrews 3:1...

⇨ What is the meaning of 'brothers and sisters'? (The Greek says 'brothers' but NIV2011 – rightly, in my opinion – has decided to translate it as 'brothers and sisters'.)

⇨ What about 'holy'? In what sense are Christians holy? (Not 'perfect' but 'set apart'.)

⇨ What does it mean to say that Jesus is 'our apostle'? ('Apostle' means 'sent one' and we usually use the word for the 12 apostles who Jesus sent out. But this writer only uses the word for Jesus, because he is the *ultimate* sent one, sent by God the Father into the world.)

⇨ And in what sense is Jesus our high priest? (In the Old Testament the high priest used to make a sacrifice for the sins of the people, so that they could be forgiven. Jesus has offered up the ultimate sacrifice – his own life on the cross – so that all who trust him are reconciled with God.)

And I will do the same with words and expressions through the whole passage. If necessary I will reach for a commentary, but I will begin by simply praying and thinking about the meaning of the words myself.

This is also the time to ask why the writer has chosen his particular combination of words. So why, in Hebrews 3:1, are we told that Jesus is apostle and high priest? Why not 'Lord and saviour' or 'shepherd and friend'?

Here is my answer to the question. As apostle, Jesus brings God to us, and as high priest he brings us to God. Everyone needs revelation and reconciliation: as apostle, Jesus brings us the revelation and as high priest he brings us the reconciliation. The combination is amazing: just writing this paragraph has got me worshipping!

d. The individual trees and the whole wood

There is nothing new to do at this point. This is just a picture to remind us of the importance of context within the passage itself. The individual trees are the words and expressions in the text, while the wood is the whole passage.

The purpose of looking at the individual words is to grasp the message of the whole passage.

Something to do (2)

Now that you have seen the process thus far with Hebrews 3:1-6, please try it yourself with another passage: John 13:1-17.

Read the passage and ask God for his help. Then grab a piece of paper or a notebook and write your answers down.

Q1. What was the original meaning?

a. Why did the writer write this book?

b. Why did he write these verses?

c. What do the individual words mean? At this point, don't think about the meaning. Just make a list of 8 or more words and expressions in the passage that you would need to think about.

d. The individual trees and the whole wood. Don't worry about this at this stage. Simply keep it in mind.

When you have written down your answers to these three questions, you can find my answers at www.howtoteachthebible.org.

Q2. What is the universal meaning?

What lessons and principles are there in this text which are true in every culture and in every century?

Let me be very clear: the meaning of a Bible text does not change. However, the original meaning is nearly always rooted in a specific historical situation which may be very different to the situation I am preaching this passage in today.

As we have seen, the Letter to the Hebrews is aimed at Jewish Christians. But let us suppose that I am teaching Hebrews 3:1-6 in a context in which there are no Jewish people. If I say "This is a wonderfully encouraging passage for Jewish Christians" most of my listeners will be thinking "Yes, but what has this got to do with me?"

So with this question "What is the universal meaning?" I am asking this: what lessons and principles are there in this text which are true in every culture and in every century?

Think for a moment about this example. 1 Corinthians 16:20b says "Greet one another with a holy kiss." I assume that Paul meant these words literally when he wrote them to the church in Corinth.

But every culture is different. It will not always be appropriate for all Christians to be kissing each other. The kissing is simply a particular cultural expression of a universal principle: Christians should show love by welcoming each other in a holy way.

This is what I mean by the universal meaning. This is about lessons and principles in a Bible passage which are true in every culture and in every century.

Let's see how this works out in Hebrews 3:1-6. As we have seen, the first readers were under pressure and were tempted to drift away from Jesus and the Gospel. These verses tell us what we can do so that instead of drifting we become increasingly passionate followers of Jesus. For example, we should fix our eyes on him (v1).

This is something that is true for every Christian in every culture and in every century. This is part of the universal meaning of this passage.

Something to do (3)

Now please turn back to John 13:1-17. As you pray, please write your answers down.

Q2. What is the universal meaning?

What lessons and principles are there in this text which are true in every culture and in every century?

When you have written down some answers to this question, you can find my answers at www.howtoteachthebible.org.

Q3. What is the application for us today?

There is a difference between meaning and application!

A lot of Bible teachers fail to get as far as application because they assume that meaning and application are the same thing.

This is a mistake.

Meaning is general principles; application is practical examples.

I once heard a sermon on the First Letter of John chapter 4, about the importance of Christians loving one another. The preacher kept repeating the sentence "We should love each other." He was right: that is part of the universal meaning of the passage.

But I wanted to stand up and shout "Tell us *how!*" The principle was clear, but there were no practical examples of what this principle might mean in practice.

As a Bible teacher myself I know that I have often made the same mistake.

Each time the preacher told us we should love one another, no one disagreed. It is clearly the teaching of the passage; if we had taken a vote everyone would have voted in favour.

But the danger is that that is where it stops.

Which is why application is so important. We need practical examples of the general principle.

This does not mean that every practical example will be relevant to every person I am speaking to. But everyone will relate to some of the applications I suggest. And something else will happen too.

Often when I am listening to preaching I react like this to a particular application: "That's not relevant to me. But hang on – in my case this will mean that I will..." – and immediately I know how I should be responding.

That is the Holy Spirit at work: he is leading me to understand what he wants me to do. This is part of experiencing preaching as a supernatural event.

But if the Bible teacher never moves from meaning to application, this may never happen. Of course the Holy Spirit can still speak to people; but it is much less likely that people will be responding to God as he speaks.

Think back to Hebrews 3:1-6. In the first verse there is a general principle – that Christians should fix their eyes on Jesus. If I tell everyone this there will be general agreement; it is self-evidently a right thing to do.

But what does it mean in practice? I need to provide some practical examples of what this might mean.

So, for instance: it means reading the Gospels, perhaps committing a Gospel passage to memory so that I can meditate on it through the day, remembering to thank Jesus that he is my apostle (he brought God to me) and my high priest (he brought me to God). You might want to add more examples.

I hope you can see how vital application is as we teach the Bible to others.

Something to do (4)

Please turn back to John 13:1-17.

Q3. What is the application for us today?

A key strand of the universal meaning of the passage is that, just as Jesus washed his disciples' feet, Christians should serve each other.

But remember this:
Meaning is general principles; application is practical examples.

So look now for practical examples of the principle. What might serving one another look like in practice?

> Imagine you are teaching pensioners. What might be some possible applications?

> Imagine you are teaching teenagers. What might be some practical applications?

When you have written down your answers, you can find my suggestions at www.howtoteachthebible.org.

Q4. What is the main thought in the passage?

Some people call this the big idea. We need to remember that there is a difference between the main thought and my favourite thought.

There are at least three reasons why the main thought is important:

a. The main thought should determine what the sermon is about.

If the Holy Spirit went to the trouble of inspiring the writer to write this passage (and he did), then with his help I want to find out why.

b. Most people forget most of any Bible talk they hear.

You have not been able to go to church today because you are unwell. When the people you share your flat with get home you ask them how the service was. Among other things you say "What was the sermon about?"

There is an awkward pause. Then comes the answer: "God." Hopefully this is true; but there is probably more that could be said!

But if the main thought of the passage (the big idea) is clear to the preacher, it will also become clear to the listeners.

c. Finding the main thought is an excellent way of checking that what you have already identified as the meaning and the application is faithful to the passage.

For this reason some Bible teachers prefer to isolate the main thought *before* thinking about meaning or application. Personally I prefer to ask this question at the end of Step One rather than at the beginning.

But do what works best for you. What is vital is *that* the question gets asked, not *when* it gets asked.

What is the main thought in Hebrews 3:1-6? Look at these three possibilities and see if you are happy with all of them:

⇨ Jesus is the greatest!

⇨ The task of a high priest.

⇨ Christians will not drift if they know that Jesus is the greatest.

We can discount the middle option straight away: the task of a high priest may be my favourite thought in the passage, but it is emphatically not the main thought.

The last option seems to me to sum up the message of these verses very well. The first option is simply an abbreviated version of it, but is perhaps too general: nearly every passage in the New Testament might be described in this way!

Although it is not always easy to identify the main thought it is really important to work at this. The big idea matters.

Something to do (5)

Turn back to John 13:1-17 and get ready to write down your answer.

Q4. What is the main thought in the passage?

Try to sum up John 13:1-17 in one sentence.

Once you have done this, you might shorten the sentence in order to create a possible title for your talk.

When you have written down your answers, you can find my suggestions at www.howtoteachthebible.org.

These four questions are Step One of preparing a sermon or Bible talk. Here is a reminder of what we have done:

Step One: Study the passage in context

Q1. What was the original meaning?

Q2. What is the universal meaning?

Q3. What is the application for us today?

Q4. What is the main thought in the passage?

I hope you will try Step One with other passages, even if you are not preparing a Bible talk.

Before we move on to Step Two, there is something else to say about this first step.

Step One is the most important step in the preparation of a Bible talk. If we get this wrong we will get everything wrong.

That is why it needs prayer and practice.

Step One: Study the passage in context

Step Two: Find a structure-with-headings

A number of questions will help us to understand what this involves.

Q1. What is a structure-with-headings?

It is a dividing-up of the Bible passage, so that there are two, three or four sections. This will depend on how the passage is written, on the flow of thought.

There should not be too many sections. A pastor in England a few centuries ago is reported as having once said the following towards the end of one of his sermons: "And now, fifty-sixthly..." If I told my listeners at the beginning of a sermon that I had fifty-six points, that would at least cause mild hysteria. And possibly mass evacuation.

Most Bible passages do break down into two, three or four sections.

Each section then needs a heading. These headings need to have two characteristics.

First, each heading must be faithful to its part of the passage. And, second, the headings must fit together so that they will be memorable.

Let me illustrate. Here are some headings which clearly do not fit together. I don't know which Bible passage this talk is about, but imagine that I have three points, as follows:

a.   God is love.

b.   When we look at Old Testament salvation history we see that it always was God's purpose to call out a people for himself who would be a light for all the nations.

c.   We should pray more.

Let us suppose that each of these headings is faithful to its part of the Bible passage. But can you see that the headings do not fit together?

Let me give you a positive example.

When I was at university about 40 years ago, a speaker came to our Christian Union and spoke about the parable of the Good Samaritan. He said that the parable showed us three different attitudes to life – the attitude of the robbers, the attitude of the religious people and the attitude of the Samaritan.

He summed them up by using these headings:

   a. "What's yours is mine, if I can get it."
   b. "What's mine is mine, if I can keep it."
   c. "What's mine is yours, if you'll accept it."

Can you see that those headings fit together? Although it was so long ago I still remember them after all these years. And my guess is that you will probably never forget them either.

So a structure-with-headings is a dividing-up of the Bible passage, where each section has its own heading. The headings should be faithful to their part of the passage, and they should fit together, too.

Q2. What are the advantages of a structure-with-headings?

a. It helps the listeners

Imagine you are reading a newspaper and discover a full-page article on a subject you are excited about. You want to read it. But if there are no paragraphs or divisions in the text and no headings of any kind apart from the headline at the top of the page, you probably decide to come back to it later.

And you may well never read it at all.

This is why sub-editors make sure there are paragraph divisions in any article and some larger breaks, each with a heading. Sometimes the headings have little or no connection to the paragraph that follows, but the fact is that an article with such divisions and headings is much more accessible: it is much more likely to be read.

It is the same with a Bible talk or a sermon.

If the listeners have been told that there are three main points coming up, they will find it easier to concentrate. And if they lose concentration at any point (because someone nearby has a coughing fit or says something to the person next to them) they will find it easier to switch on again, because they will know which point the speaker has reached.

In addition, a good structure-with-headings will be memorable for the listeners. This means that they can preach a short version of the sermon to themselves again and in this way meditate more easily on the Bible passage. In short, they will be more likely to put what God has said into practice.

b. It helps the speaker

When I first started to preach I was 20 years old. I had never had any training about how to go about preparing to teach a Bible passage.

I would read the passage and pray. I then wrote down all the thoughts and ideas which occurred to me: the meaning of words and phrases, examples or stories which would help me explain things, good applications of whatever the Bible passage was teaching.

But then I was stuck.

I didn't know what to do next. I had this sheet of A4 covered with ideas, stories and applications – which is basically Step One of the method I am teaching in this book.

But what now?

I did not have an answer to that question. So I used to preach with this sheet of A4 in front of me, and you can imagine how jumbled and confused everything was. I am relieved that recordings of my early sermons are unavailable!

I still fill up a sheet of A4 as I do Step One. But now I go on to Step Two: I start to look for a structure-with-headings. This is a massive help to me in my preparation.

But not only that.

The structure-with-headings also helps me while I am giving my talk. It helps me to be clear. And I also know how far I have got: if I have three points and I am still on the first after 12 minutes of preaching, I know that I need to get moving.

I can no longer imagine giving a Bible talk without having a structure-with-headings. If you are doubtful about the value of this, I beg you to keep reading and at least give it a try.

The Holy Spirit may have a surprise for you.

Q3. What can be the disadvantages of a structure-with-headings?

Of course it is possible that it misuses the Bible text because I have imposed a structure which is foreign to the passage.

Or perhaps the headings are not faithful to their parts of the text.

If either of these two things happens, this is no longer exposition, but imposition. Instead of bringing out what the Holy Spirit has put into the passage I am putting things into the passage which I have come up with myself.

So there are dangers.

But there is a remedy too. The main thought – or the big idea – must influence and shape the structure-with-headings.

Q4. How can I find a structure-with-headings?

Very often it is possible to divide up a Bible passage into two or three paragraphs or blocks of thought.

Sometimes the paragraph divisions in the translations will help with this, but we need to remember that the paragraphing is not in the original but simply the suggestion of the translators.

Certain words can help us to identify the beginning of a new block of thought. "But" at the beginning of a sentence is an immediate clue, for example. And if a sentence begins with the word "therefore", it is either the beginning of a new thought or the end of an old one.

The structure-with-headings might be

a. three principles (most likely in a teaching passage, for example from one of the New Testament letters);

b. three descriptions of what happens in the text (this works best for a narrative passage, for example a Gospel or an Old Testament historical narrative);

c. three questions (where each section answers the question in its heading);

d. three answers to one question (you ask a question in your introduction and the three sections provide the answers).

But why 3 sections and 3 headings?!?!?

We have all heard jokes about three-point sermons! *And of course if the Bible passage has two or four parts the sermon needs the corresponding number of parts.* But many passages really do have a three-part structure.

And there is something about the number 3.

Why do many jokes work best with the number 3? Here is an example:

Two boys are writing an exam in school. Their teacher is checking that they are not cheating. He says to one of the boys: "You're looking at this other boy's answers!" The boy denies it. "Look at the two answer sheets," says the teacher.

"He's written 'Number 1: Yes'; you've written 'Number 1: Yes.'

He's written 'Number 2: No'; you've written 'Number 2: No.'

He's written 'Number 3: I don't know'; you've written 'Number 3: Neither do I.'"

Trust me: if you tell that joke and put the punch-line with Number 2 or with Number 4, you will get much less of a laugh. There is something about the number 3.

Why is the number 3 special to us? I don't know if it has something to do with the fact that we have been created in the image of a God who is a trinity; but there is no doubt that there is something about the number 3.

Q5. How did I find a structure-with-headings for Hebrews 3:1-6?

This is the main thought for this passage:

Christians will not drift if they know that Jesus is the greatest.

My main problem in preparation was verses 2-6a, which is a huge problem because it is more than half of the passage. Verse 1 seemed clear, as did the second half of verse 6.

But what were verses 2-6a about?

As I read, thought and prayed, it became clear to me that what is happening in these central verses is that the writer is comparing Moses, the first readers' great hero, with Jesus.

And showing that Jesus is better.

And so my structure-with-headings for Hebrews 3:1-6 ended up like this. It is three answers to a question.

Hebrews 3:1-6 / Structure-with-headings

The question: what can we do so that we will not drift away from Jesus?

The answers:
1. Look! (1)
2. Compare! (2-6a)
3. Hold on! (6b)

I don't consider this structure-with-headings to be stunning.

But I do think each heading is faithful to its part of the passage; and the headings do fit together (although, because I am picky about these things, I would prefer the third heading to contain one word rather than two!).

And having a structure-with-headings makes it easier for me to teach this Bible passage so that people meet God.

Something to do (6)

Please turn back to John 13:1-17. I hope you will try Step Two.

First, divide up the passage into 2, 3 or 4 sections, *without trying to think of any headings.*

Second (and only after you have decided what the structure is), try to find headings with the following characteristics:
Each must be faithful to its part of the passage.
The headings must fit together.

Please note:

a. Don't be satisfied with just one set of headings – find as many as you can and then choose the best.

b. Use the list of possibilities in Question 4 on page 29 to give you ideas for your headings.

c. Be creative! While there is no room for creativity in Step One (the creativity there is all the Holy Spirit's as he inspired the human author), we can be very creative in Step Two.

d. There are some ideas on the website which will help you find a structure-with-headings. See www.howtoteachthebible.org.

When you have written down your answers, you can find my suggestions at www.howtoteachthebible.org.

I hope you have enjoyed working on a structure-with-headings. If you do not try this out and practise it, you will never discover how extraordinarily helpful it is – both to you as you teach and to others as they listen.

As we approach the end of Step Two, there are some more questions which we need to look at.

Q6. What makes for a bad structure-with-headings?

It doesn't matter how brilliant your headings are if the structure you have come up with involves a twisting of the Bible passage.

So when starting to divide up the text into a number of sections it is important to be asking the Holy Spirit for his help. And, if I am uncertain, I will ask a couple of friends what they think about the structure before I go on to look for headings.

It is important not to rush into the search for headings until I am as sure as I can be that I have found the structure of the passage.

Sometimes a structure-with-headings is poor because of shortcomings in the headings rather than in the structure. Maybe each heading is not faithful to its part of the text or the headings do not fit together.

Everyone has their own view about alliteration. Is it good if all the headings begin with the same letter?

I have no problem with alliteration *unless it is forced and artificial.* If it is natural and the words used can be easily understood, that is fine; but if one of the headings uses an expression that is unnatural simply because of the letter it begins with, then alliteration in that case is producing a bad structure-with-headings.

Think again for a moment of my structure-with-headings for Hebrews 3:1-6:

1. Look! (1)
2. Compare! (2-6a)
3. Hold on! (6b)

I might decide to see if I can find headings which all begin with the same letter. I could use 'Consider' for the first point. But then I would get stuck. And I might end up with something like this:

1. Consider! (1)
2. Compare! (2-6a)
3. Clasp! (6b)

I don't know about you, but I think the third heading is artificial and weak. It will distract the listeners rather than helping them to focus on what God is saying.

Alliteration is great when it works; otherwise it should be avoided at all costs.

There is one other thing that makes for a bad structure-with-headings: overloaded headings. That is, the Bible teacher has tried to find headings which include as many details of the passage as possible. The problem with this is that the headings become cumbersome and will not be remembered by the listeners.

Here is what overloaded headings might look like with Hebrews 3:1-6:

1. Look at Jesus our apostle and high priest (1)
2. Compare Jesus and Moses – you will find that Jesus is better (2-6a)
3. Hold on to our confidence and hope (6b)

I hope you can see that there is too much content in the headings. And in this case the overloading has also resulted in the headings not really fitting together.

Q7. What makes for a good structure-with-headings?

The whole of Step Two has been providing answers to this question. But something is worth adding here which is particularly helpful if you are dealing with a narrative passage.

In general it is good to use a verb rather than a noun. So a heading like "Jesus' action" is often much better if it becomes "What Jesus did".

And if you are using a verb in a structure-with-headings, the present tense is better than the past, because it engages the imagination of the listener much more. So, better than "What Jesus did" would be "What Jesus does".

Q8. How should I use a structure-with-headings?

Remember that the structure-with-headings is not only helpful for you as the Bible teacher; it is also helpful for the listeners.

But that means you need to *use* your headings, and not keep them to yourself! If I catch myself hardly using my headings this is almost always because I am a bit embarrassed by them. Either I have a suspicion that they are not faithful to the Bible passage, or I know that they don't fit together.

Using my headings will make for clearer communication.

But that does not mean that I give my listeners all the headings at the beginning of the sermon. If I do that I am giving the game away; and while I am then talking about my first point some people are going to be wondering why I chose that heading for my third point!

Let's take Hebrews 3:1-6 as an example again.

In my introduction I will say that there are three things we can do to stop us drifting away from Jesus. Then I will say: "First, in verse 1, *look*." Now I talk about the second half of verse 1.

Then, at the end of that point I will say: "So that's the first thing we can do: *look*. Now, second, in verse 2 to the beginning of verse 6, *compare*."

At the end of my second point I will say: "So we've seen two things we can do to stop ourselves drifting away from Jesus: *look* and *compare*. Now, third, in the second half of verse 6, *hold on*."

Forgive me if I am labouring the point. But I do think this is important. I am not going to tell everyone my headings at the beginning of my sermon, but I *am* going to use them. By the time I have finished I would like everyone to be able to remember what my headings were.

Q9. Why should I bother with a structure-with-headings?

Some Bible teachers ask this question because they feel that finding a structure-with-headings requires too much effort.

But I am convinced that it is worth it.

If you have a huge teaching gift you can get away without a structure-with-headings: people will listen to you even if you are just reading out extracts from the phone book!

I can think of a few preachers who are hugely gifted and who do not use a structure-with-headings and it doesn't seem to matter. As they listen people are still meeting God. But I dare to add this: afterwards the listeners will have trouble communicating clearly to others the content of what they have just heard.

And often hugely gifted Bible teachers will still use a structure-with-headings because they know it will help the listeners. The two models I mentioned in Part One fall into this category.

But for those of us with a teaching gift which is not extraordinary a structure-with-headings will be a massive help.

Personally I could not do without it.

Q10. How can I get better at finding a structure-with-headings?

The first thing to do is to practise.

Alan, a sixteen-year-old boy who was a Christian at an English boarding school, tried the experiment of meeting up with a few other Christian boys before school on three days in the week. They would read a Bible passage and then Alan would explain it to the group by dividing it up and giving a heading to each part.

Since none of the other boys wanted to try doing this teaching, Alan ended up doing it himself for two years.

He went on to become one of the clearest Bible teachers in England.[1]

If you want to become better at finding a structure-with-headings you need to practise. You can try this even if you are not going to give a talk on the Bible passage. When I am reading the Bible I often look for a structure-with-headings.

That is one reason why I find it easier to find a structure-with-headings now than I used to.

And the second thing to do is to pray. If you are serious about wanting to teach the Bible, ask God to increase your ability to discover the structure of a passage and then find headings that help people hear God speaking through the Bible.

If we don't ask, we don't get (James 4:2b).

If we practise and pray we will grow in the gift of teaching. And the goal will motivate us: we long for people to experience Bible teaching and preaching as a supernatural event – an encounter with God himself.

Something to do (7)

Why not try to find a structure-with-headings for some or all of the following passages?

a. Mark 8:27-38
b. Ephesians 2:1-10
c. Philippians 1:3-26
d. 1 Corinthians 9:19-27
e. Luke 5:1-11

First, divide up the passage into 2, 3 or 4 sections, *without trying to think of any headings.*

---

[1] From Alan M. Stibbs: *Understanding, Expounding and Obeying God's Word*, pp. 74-75, Authentic Media 2009.

Second (and only after you have decided what the structure is), try to find headings with the following characteristics:

each must be faithful to its part of the passage;
the headings must fit together.

And please be praying as you do this.

As you work at finding a structure-with-headings, you are doing Step Two. But you will notice that you are doing Step One at the same time: it is impossible to look for a structure-with-headings without studying the passage at the same time. Doing Step Two forces you to do Step One.

When you have written down your answers, you can find my comments and suggestions regarding each of those passages at www.howtoteach thebible.org.

One last thought about the structure-with-headings. Although, as I have already said, Step One (Study the passage in context) is the most important stage in the preparation of a Bible talk, I have found that Step Two (Find a structure-with-headings) often takes longer than either of the other two steps.

It is usually not so difficult to find the structure of the text. But I want to take time to find headings which really are faithful to the passage *and* which will stick in the memory of the listeners so that they will meditate on what the Holy Spirit has been saying to them.

And meet God.

Step One: Study the passage in context
Step Two: Find a structure-with-headings
Step Three: Add the flesh and the blood

After Step Two I have a skeleton – just a structure-with-headings. Now it is time to add the flesh and the blood.

The flesh is the biblical content; the blood is the emotion and the fire.

Every Bible talk needs an introduction, a main body and a conclusion. It is usually better to write the introduction and the conclusion *after* you have prepared the main body of the talk.

1. The main body

Here I need to ask myself three questions.

a. What must I explain?

This is the first task of any Bible teacher. If I am not explaining the passage I am not doing my job properly.

b. What examples could I use?

I once heard John Stott saying that one of his weaknesses as a preacher was the lack of examples. He told us about a friend of his who said "John, I've read your latest book. It's excellent, but it's like a room without windows."

Examples and illustrations are like windows. Without them, the listeners are in the dark.

But examples can be dangerous.

Sometimes, when I cannot think of a good example, I am tempted to use an example which is not relevant, perhaps one of my favourite stories. This is a massive mistake because it will draw the listeners *away* from the message of the text instead of taking them *to* it.

If I cannot think of a good, relevant example, it is better not to use one at all.

Of all the other dangers I will only mention one. If Bible teachers use examples from their own lives they need to be careful: some illustrations not only explain the text (which is good) but also put the speaker in an incredibly positive light (which is bad). The goal of my Bible teaching is not that people admire me but that they admire God.

c. What application will I bring?

It is important to be asking this question the whole time.

With some Bible passages it will be more natural to leave all the application until the end. For others, particularly teaching passages from the New Testament letters, it will make much more sense to apply the lessons at the end of each point before going on to the next.

Let's see how these three questions help me to prepare the main body of the talk on Hebrews 3:1-6.

---

1. Look! (v1)

a. What must I explain?

Look / fix your eyes upon.

Apostle (sent one).

High priest (who brings a sacrifice).

As apostle Jesus brings God to us, as high priest he brings us to God.

b. What examples could I use?

The example of the girl-friend's photo.
(This illustrates what is meant by looking fixedly.)

c. What application will I bring?

(Because this is a teaching passage and my main points are principles or lessons, it is natural to apply at the end of each point.)

Quiet Time.

Thinking during the day about Jesus the apostle and high priest.

Memorising a passage from the Gospels and using that to help me look at Jesus.

I write all this on one piece of paper. Now, on another piece of paper…

2. Compare! (v2-6a)

a. What must I explain?

The background in Numbers 12:7.
('House' is a way of referring to God's people.)

The comparisons between Moses and Jesus.
(I will probably list these at this stage.)

b. What examples could I use?

Examples of things which could pull us away from God: the old religion, a sin, a friendship, anything which seems more important to us.

c. What application will I bring?

Think about what is pulling you away from God, and spend time comparing it with Jesus.

And on a third piece of paper...

3. Hold on! (6b)

a. What must I explain?

Confidence. (In Hebrews this means the confidence of knowing we have the right to go into the presence of God – see also 4:16 and 10:19.)

Hope. (Being sure that one day God will take us home to be with him.)

Hold on.

b. What examples could I use?

The Queen, Prince Charles, and me.

Two Christians praying.

c. What application will I bring?

Our own prayer lives.

Practise holding on to our confidence when we pray this coming week.

So I now have three pieces of paper for the three points of the main body of the sermon. I am not going to have these in front of me when I preach; but they will be a huge help when I come to write my final notes (see 4, on page 46).

The notes you have just looked at will make much more sense if you listen to this talk online. Go to www.howtoteachthebible.org. You could listen to it now or you might decide to wait until the end of Part Two of this book.

Something to do (8)

Please turn back to John 13:1-17.

Decide on which structure-with-headings you are going to use. It is up to you whether you use the one you came up with yourself or one you found at www.howtoteachthebible.org.

Now, having seen how I prepared the main body for Hebrews 3:1-6, use the same three questions for each point of your talk on John 13:1-17:

a. What must I explain?

b. What examples could I use?

c. What application will I bring? (But remember that with a narrative passage you *may* want to leave the application till the end.)

When you have written down your answers, you can find an example of my own at www.howtoteachthebible.org.

---

2. The introduction

During the introduction the listeners make a decision. And you know what the decision is, because you do exactly the same when someone else is teaching the Bible!

Am I going to listen to this or not?

Rumour has it that some people make this decision during the first 30 seconds of the Bible talk. Somehow we need to grab their attention and convince them that it is worth their while to listen.

The best way to do this is to build a bridge between the Bible text and the life of the listeners. There is no point in waiting till the main body of the sermon to do this: I have to do it in the introduction.

This means, of course, that I will need to think about the kind of people I will be speaking to.

So here is what the introduction for Hebrews 3:1-6 might look like:

Hebrews 3:1-6 / Introduction

The first readers were tempted to drift away from Jesus... (the Bible text).

We face similar temptations... (the life of the listeners) and there are three things in this passage which will help us not to drift.

I hope you can see how that builds the bridge: it shows the listeners (if they are Christians) that this is exactly the passage they need if they want to grow in passion for Jesus instead of drifting away from him.

It is up to you to decide *from which end* you will build the bridge.

Sometimes you might start with the Bible text and then explain how relevant that is to us today; sometimes you will begin with an issue which many of us face or struggle with and then explain how this Bible passage is exactly what we need.

Usually we grab people's attention more quickly if we use the second of those two options. But the vital thing is to build the bridge.

But in the case of Hebrews 3:1-6, the introduction is not finished yet. If we look at verse 1 the reason will be clear.

"Therefore, holy brothers and sisters, who share in the heavenly calling, *fix your thoughts on Jesus, whom we acknowledge as our apostle and high priest.*"

I have italicised my first point: "Look!" I hope you can see that every-thing that comes before that, because it is not part of the first point, actually belongs in the introduction.

So here is the introduction again. You will notice that I am now building the bridge from the other end and that I have added something to the end of my introduction...

Hebrews 3:1-6 / Introduction

We all face the temptation to give up following Jesus (the life of the listeners).

The first readers faced the same temptation (the Bible text); and there are three things in this passage which will help us not to drift.

But before we look at them, let's notice how the writer describes Christians (v1a).

So now let's look at the three things in this passage which will help us not to drift...

If the introduction is too long, some of the listeners will switch off. And if the introduction is too short, some of the listeners will not have switched on.

I realise that that last paragraph is somewhat unhelpful! Let me try to do better.

Bible teachers have differing opinions about this, but here is a rule of thumb. If I am preaching for 30 minutes, I think my introduction should last no longer than 5 minutes (3 or 4 minutes would be better).

This matters, but the most important thing to say about the introduction is that it must build the bridge.

Something to do (9)

Please turn back to John 13:1-17.

Now write some notes for an introduction to your talk. Remember to build the bridge between the lives of the listeners and the Bible passage.

You might try two versions. First, build the bridge starting with the Bible passage; second, build the bridge starting with the lives of the listeners.

When you have written down your answers, you can find my suggestions at www.howtoteachthebible.org.

3. The conclusion

The talk should reach a climax. A conclusion offers a fantastic opportunity to increase the impact of what you have said by repeating the most important things.

The conclusion should be short: this is not the time to repeat the whole sermon!

Imagine you have been learning to fly a plane. You have done all the training, and today is the first time you will fly a plane with passengers in it. You are understandably nervous.

Taking off and flying are no problem. It's landing that is difficult. Time and again you are approaching the runway, ready to land, but lose courage at the last minute – and suddenly the plane is up above the clouds again.

Some preachers are like that. They find it really hard to land.

I know this because I have experienced this problem myself. I have been teaching and I am into my conclusion. But while I am talking I am thinking "Actually, Andrew, you wanted to stop now. But you don't know how." So I just keep talking.

And the whole church is willing me to land!

So it is worthwhile choosing your words carefully. Whatever kind of notes you plan to use while you are speaking, I recommend that you write your conclusion out in full. Not that you will read it; but the fact that you have thought through how to finish will mean that you will experience a successful landing.

Sometimes a good example or a good story (if it is not too long) will help. When preparing Hebrews 3:1-6 I could think of three examples for my third point (which is unusual for me), so I kept one of them back for my conclusion.

And often it is natural to have something in the conclusion which links back to the introduction. For the listeners this increases the sense that what the Holy Spirit has said through the Bible passage really has dealt with the issue you introduced at the beginning of your talk.

Hebrews 3:1-6 / Conclusion

Look, compare and hold on.

Example: the sign on the bus.

Keep going till the end.

Something to do (10)

Turn back to John 13:1-17 for a few minutes.

Write out a short, clear conclusion to your Bible talk.

When you have written down your conclusion, you can find a suggestion from me at www.howtoteachthebible.org.

There is one more important thing to say about the conclusion. I recommend that you pray at the end of your Bible talk.

If you don't do it, it may not happen at all or someone else may lead in prayer in a way that misses the point of the passage.

And Satan is laughing.

If you do do it, you are giving all your listeners the opportunity to respond to what the Holy Spirit has been saying through his word. You might start with a time of quiet, in which you encourage everyone to pray in silence, before you lead in a short, final prayer.

And God is rejoicing.

But where's the blood?

The third step of the method I am teaching here is called **Add the flesh and the blood.** I explained that like this:

The flesh is the biblical content; the blood is the emotion and the fire.

In looking at the introduction, the main body of the Bible talk, and the conclusion we have been talking about the flesh.

So where's the blood?

What I cannot do is teach you ways of being passionate and emotional. Some people will try to do it, but you will end up not being you.

What I can do is encourage you to do all your preparation and all your teaching as worship to God. Open yourself up to the Holy Spirit: allow him to use truth to touch you and move you.

If your preparation is just academic, your teaching will be just academic too. But if you are meeting God as you prepare, that will come through in your teaching.

Emotion and fire are key elements in Bible teaching. But these need to come through in a way that is natural to you.

It would be good to talk to your mentor about this.

Which is another reason why Part Three of this book is so important.

4. Writing good notes

a. Notes must be clear

It is stating the obvious to say that our notes need to be clear. But there are some Bible teachers whose teaching is muddled because their notes are muddled.

However you write your notes, make sure they are clear. While you are speaking you don't want to be thinking "What on earth did I mean by this sentence?" Instead *you want to be able to concentrate on the passage, the listeners and the Lord.*

b. How I started

When I began to do Bible teaching someone advised me to write out every word during the first year. This worked well. Usually I didn't find that I had to read them; because I had done the work of writing them out, I was able to express myself clearly while only referring to the notes from time to time.

Later I was advised to write it all out in full, but then to write shorter notes to speak from. I really struggled with this: it was difficult for me, as an inexperienced preacher, to go off to the meeting without the full notes that I had worked so hard to write.

But sometimes I managed it.

c. My next step

The time came when I found a method of note-writing which served me well for the next 20 years. I recommend that you try it, even if you then decide on something else that works better for you.

This method involves writing not full notes but notes which you could read out in an emergency – in other words, if your mind just goes blank.

Start each main thought on the left and indent everything else. This means that when it is time for a new main thought you know where to find it: on the left.

Here is an idea of what that might look like...

Hebrews 3:1-6 / Introduction

When was the last time you said this?

"I give up. Following Jesus is too much effort. I give up."

That was exactly the situation the first readers of this letter were in.

They were Jews who had become Christians.

But they were under pressure; there was persecution;

and they felt like giving up following Jesus and going back to the old religion.

Now the writer of this letter is writing to help them not give up.

He wants them to stay passionate about Jesus.

So in this passage at the beginning of chapter 3 he gives them 3 things they can do which will help them keep going as Christians.

And if we ever feel like giving up following Jesus, these things can help us too.

But before we look at them, just see how the writer of this letter describes Christians...

I hope you can see that this works. If I know what each paragraph is about I can talk freely, without having to read the notes out. But when I have finished one thought and need a reminder about what the next one is, I know where to look: on the left.

It works. Try preaching that Hebrews 3 introduction for yourself, if you like – out loud.

But not on the bus.

d. Your own notes

Maybe you will decide to preach with a full text. That is fine. I know some Bible teachers who preach with every word in their notes, but you would never know it.

Or perhaps you will try for briefer notes. That is fine too, provided you can be clear.

But whatever notes you decide to teach with, there are two things worth stressing.

First, use the right size of paper. If you are teaching in a pulpit or at a lectern you will find that there is sometimes not enough space for your Bible *and* for a collection of A4 notes.

I have solved this problem by having paper that is the same size as one page in my Bible. This way I always have space. And if there is no pulpit or lectern (or I don't want to use one), I can simply hold my Bible in my hands, with the notes on top of it.

Second, number the pages clearly. If you do this, you will know that you have everything in the right order. That way *you will be able to concentrate on the passage, the listeners and the Lord.*

When it comes to preparing a sermon or Bible talk we need a method which is simple. So this is what we have looked at:

Part Two: A Method

1. **Study the passage in context**

2. **Find a structure-with-headings**

3. **Add the flesh and the blood**

Of course you may decide to do some things rather differently from the way I suggest. But I hope you will try all three steps nevertheless.

In my experience many people are sceptical about Step Two: Find a structure-with-headings. But most people change their minds once they have tried it for themselves.

We will not grow as Bible teachers if we do not study, experiment and pray.

I hope you will do all three.

Part Three

A Mentor

So you have identified one or two Bible teaching models. And I have taught you a method of preparing to preach a Bible passage.

The next stage is to find a mentor.

But I want to introduce Part Three by reminding you of why I think it is so important that the method is simple. This is because Christians with the gift of teaching will often instinctively know things about teaching that they have never been taught.

So you don't need to tell most people with a teaching gift that it is important to use sentences that are not too long – it seems to them to be obvious.

And you don't need to tell people with a teaching gift that a psalm must be preached differently from a Gospel passage or a section from one of the New Testament letters – it seems to them to be obvious.

So there is no need for the method to explain these things.

But of course we all have blind spots. This is why every Bible-teacher needs a mentor, someone who can help them to grow in their gift.

That is what Part Three is about.

1. What should a mentor be like?

I suggest you look for someone who is a more experienced Bible teacher than you are, and whose Bible teaching you respect, admire and have been blessed by.

Perhaps this person is even one of the model Bible teachers you came up with in Part One of this book.

If you are more or less sticking to the method described in Part Two, it is important that the person you ask to be your mentor understands what you are trying to do.

Make sure, too, that your mentor believes that growing as a Bible teacher is not just a matter of practice, but that it is the result of prayer. It is the Holy Spirit who equips God's people so that by using the gifts he has given them they can glorify Jesus.

So find a mentor who wants to pray for you and with you.

2. How can I find out if I have the gift of teaching?

I am asking this question in Part Three, because often a mentor will see things in us that we cannot see in ourselves.

The gift of teaching is mentioned in the lists of spiritual gifts in the New Testament (see Romans 12:7, 1 Corinthians 12:28, Ephesians 4:11 and 1 Peter 4:11). Every Christian has been given at least one spiritual gift by the Holy Spirit: no one has no gifts, no one has all the gifts, no gift is given to every Christian.

So how can I find out if I have the gift of teaching?

One way is simply to start teaching the Bible whenever I get the opportunity, whether to one friend or to a group of people.

I did not find out whether I had the gift of playing tennis by reading books about it and watching Wimbledon. No, I actually started playing tennis.

And it did not take very long before I realised that I do *not* have the gift of playing tennis!

So if you want to find out if the Holy Spirit has given you the gift of teaching, start asking God for opportunities to teach. But there is something else you can do too.

Below are five indications that the Holy Spirit has given someone the gift of teaching. You don't have to have all five characteristics in order to know that God wants you to be a Bible teacher; but if you have none of these it may well be that you do not have the gift of teaching and should be concentrating on using other gifts as you serve God.[2]

As you look at these characteristics or discuss them with your mentor, you may experience a sense of rising excitement. Or the opposite.

In any case we will all have some things to pray about.

---

[2] The 5 characteristics are from a lecture by Bill Hybels, and adapted by the author.

a. A Christian with the gift of teaching enjoys preparation

This means that the idea of sitting down, praying, and starting to study a Bible passage with a view to teaching it to others is positive for you.

This does not mean that there will not be times when you get stuck and wonder if you are ever going to get your preparation finished.

But the prospect and experience of preparation gives you a buzz.

b. A Christian with the gift of teaching believes that what God uses more than anything else to change lives is the Bible

Of course he uses other things too: worship, counselling, friendship, prayer.

But I am convinced that he uses the Bible more than anything else.

If I am not convinced of this I will not take the time to pray, read and prepare.

c. A Christian with the gift of teaching knows the at-the-same-time experience

When Christians with the gift of teaching learn something from God in the Bible, they have two experiences at the same time.

First, they thank God for what they have learnt.

And second, they immediately find themselves thinking things like this: "I must show this to Tina" or "This would fit really well into the talk I'm doing at the youth group next week."

In other words, at the same time as they are learning something they are immediately thinking of people they can pass it on to. This is the at-the-same-time experience.

I used to think that all Christians had this experience. But they don't. And that is because most Christians have other spiritual gifts.

d. A Christian with the gift of teaching receives positive, honest feedback

In other words, when you teach people give you positive reactions.

But it does have to be honest. If someone tells you "I think you are more gifted than the apostle Paul," don't take it seriously.

You aren't. Trust me.

Positive and honest feedback might look like this: "I thought your introduction was a bit confusing, but when you started talking about the cross it was all so clear and I found myself worshipping." That is positive and honest.

I once heard a student from England preaching in a tiny church in Wales. He had obviously never had any basic training in how to teach the Bible. It wasn't just his hands that were shaking; his voice was shaking too.

He put his notes on the floor and read the passage from his Bible. Then he put his Bible on the floor, picked up his notes and began to preach. When he said "Listen to what Jesus says in verse 23," he put his notes back on the floor, picked up his Bible again and read the verse.

And so on. You get the idea. No points for technique.

But, thirty years or so later, I still remember the Bible passage and how God spoke to me through it.

After the service I thanked him for the sermon. He grimaced. "Was that your first time preaching?" I asked.

"Yes," he replied. "And it was my last time, too."

I remember saying that of course there was lots he could learn about how to teach the Bible. But, I said, he had let God speak through the passage. I told him that of course I had only heard him teach the Bible once, but that I thought it was quite possible that he had the gift of teaching.

So I encouraged him to look for more opportunites to teach the Bible.

It would be great if I could finish this story by saying "And that young man is now pastoring a church with a membership of 9,000 people."

But I can't. Perhaps he has never tried to teach the Bible to others since that day. Or perhaps he is now a Bible teacher God is using to help people have a divine encounter.

I hope you see what I mean by positive, honest feedback.

e. A Christian with the gift of teaching knows the inner witness of the Holy Spirit

This is a very subjective experience. When I began to teach the Bible I would say I knew very little of this witness.

But it has grown over the years.

In my first year of preaching, when I was at university and being invited to speak in tiny country chapels with seven or eight people in the congregation, I often had a sense of failure after I had preached.

On one occasion I got back to my room and told the Lord I never wanted to preach again, because that had been public humiliation and I obviously didn't have the gift of teaching.

A couple of weeks later I was invited to preach in another chapel. I heard myself reply "Fine. Tell me the date, the time and the address. And is there a Bible passage?"

When I had put the phone down I realised what I had done.

I had said "Yes" because something in me – or, more correctly, some*one* in me – was pushing me in the direction of teaching the Bible. I *wanted* to do it.

That is the inner witness of the Holy Spirit.

Jeremiah once heard this message: "Is not my word like fire, declares the LORD, and like a hammer that breaks a rock in pieces?" (Jeremiah 23:29)

If you have the inner witness of the Holy Spirit – even the beginnings of it – you will want, with his help, to teach the word of God to others.

Something to do (11)

Take a few minutes to pray through these five characteristics of a Christian with the gift of teaching. They are not infallible, but they are helpful.

A Christian with the gift of teaching

a. enjoys preparation;

b. believes that what God uses more than anything else to change lives is the Bible;

c. knows the at-the-same-time experience;

d. receives positive, honest feedback;

e. knows the inner witness of the Holy Spirit.

Which of these characteristics do you see in yourself?

Do you want to ask God to make any of these characteristics grow in you?

If you have a mentor, why not chat these things through with them?

3. How can your mentor help you grow?

a. By helping you prepare a talk

If you have been working through this book with a friend you will already have experienced how strengthening it is to have input from somebody else.

You could either prepare a talk together or you could ask them for help at various stages of your preparation.

b. By giving you feedback

There are four questions which will help any mentor provide feedback on a sermon or Bible talk. And the answers will help you become a better Bible teacher.

Here they are...

Was it faithful? (Was it true to the content of the passage?)

Was it clear? (Did it have a structure which made sense and headings which communicated clearly?)

Was it relevant? (Did the introduction build the bridge between the text and the listeners? Did the application consist of vague generalisations or of practical suggestions?)

Did it glorify God? or *Did it glorify Jesus?* (Did the talk make us admire God and/or Jesus more?)[3]

---

[3] The first three questions are to be found in Jonathan Lamb: *Preaching Matters,* pp. 181-182, InterVarsity Press 2014.

Of course your mentor may want to give feedback about other things too. For example: the fact that you never look at the listeners, or the way you pick your nose, or your habit of saying "OK?" every few minutes, or the way you show no passion while talking about the love of God.

But the essential ingredients are the answers to the four questions.

c. By running a Bible Teachers' Club for you and for others

A Bible Teachers' Club consists of between three and six people who either know they have the gift of teaching or want to find out if they do. They agree to meet, say, four times.

They decide to preach through the Letter to the Philippians (rather than Ezekiel or Revelation). Leave more difficult Bible books for later.

At each 90-minute meeting the following happens:

Someone opens in prayer.

One group member, who has prepared a 15-minute talk on Philippians 1:1-11, gives the talk.

After saying some positive things about the talk, the others answer the four questions:

> *Was it faithful?*
> *Was it clear?*
> *Was it relevant?*
> *Did it glorify God / Jesus?*

Another group-member, who has prepared a 15-minute talk on Philippians 1:12-26, gives the talk.

After saying some positive things about the talk, the others answer the four questions:

> *Was it faithful?*
> *Was it clear?*
> *Was it relevant?*
> *Did it glorify God / Jesus?*

They then pray together for one another, and also for Bible teaching in their country.

A Bible Teachers' Club has the following rules:

> If you join the Bible Teachers' Club you are agreeing to come to all the meetings.

> If you join the Bible Teachers' Club you are agreeing to do one or more of the Bible talks. (There is no such thing as observer status.)

If those who are functioning as mentors can help in the creation of Bible Teachers' Clubs, they will be helping all those involved and blessing the church, both locally and more widely.

Something to do (12)

Have a think about these questions, and write the answers down:

Do you already have someone who is mentoring you as you teach the Bible?

Do you have someone in mind?

Would you like to be involved in a Bible Teachers' Club?

If so, how might you go about setting one up?

Pray for a few minutes about what you have written down.

Conclusion

How to Help People Meet God

There is power in the word of God.

Bible teaching is not only about information. It is about encounter. If you have ever had the experience of knowing that God was speaking to you through the Bible, then you long for others to hear God too.

So, in conclusion, here are some suggestions of things to do which may make it more likely that our preaching can become a supernatural event.

1. Encourage people to do two things at once

If I am teaching the Bible I want to invite my listeners to be reading and listening, and *at the same time* to be talking to God.

I believe this is the missing ingredient in many Christians' understanding of preaching.

I have read many books about preaching and benefited greatly from them. But I cannot remember ever reading this idea of doing two things at once.

If you are simply reading and listening as someone is teaching the Bible, you are in listening-to-a-lecture mode. To some Christians this is a foreign concept, while for others it is just plain unhealthy.

Of course the purpose of preaching is to teach people the word of God. But if this is all that happens, I am bitterly disappointed.

Sometimes a service leader says something like this: "After this next song we are going to have our Bible reading, and then Andrew Page is going to come and explain the passage."

I certainly want to explain the passage. If I fail to do that I am not doing my job as a Bible teacher.

But is that all? Is my preaching only about the transmission of information?

Now of course I cannot create an encounter with God. But what I can do – with the Spirit's help – is play my part in creating a situation in which it is more likely that people will meet God.

And a key part of that is encouraging people to pray, and to keep praying, as they hear the word of God.

As a Bible teacher I try to do two things at once too. At the same time as I speak the word of God I want to be able to be asking God to speak into the hearts of my listeners.

Sometimes this is easy. I am able to pray for individuals, pray for those who are very weighed down, and pray for the Holy Spirit to speak intimately into the depths of people's personalities.

So that they know that they are meeting God.

And sometimes I can't do it at all. I feel like I am struggling to communicate without losing my train of thought, things are distracting me and I am not enjoying teaching the Bible.

This does not mean, of course, that God is at work in the first situation and not in the second!

But, just as I invite my listeners to be doing two things at once, I want to try to do two things at once, too.

2. Avoid giving a lecture

There are three things which easily make Bible teaching into the giving and hearing of a lecture.

There is a place for lectures. It's called a lecture theatre. But the preacher is not called to be a lecturer.

So here are three things to be wary of. It is your decision what you choose to do with them.

a. Standing in a pulpit

I may need to stand in a pulpit in order for people to be able to see me easily. But if possible I will avoid it.

Standing in a pulpit – or at a lectern – puts me in a position of authority. In a postmodern culture that is not going to be a help for many of my listeners.

It is not going to help them to hear God speak.

Of course authority is important in the Church. But not the authority of the Bible teacher, but the authority of God speaking through the Bible.

b. Over-use of notes

We have already thought about the value of clear notes which enable the Bible teacher to concentrate on the listeners, on the Bible and on the Lord (see pages 46-48).

For some preachers it is a massive help to have a full script of what they plan to say. But if they end up reading it word for word it becomes a lecture.

In the last few years I have experimented with preaching without notes. I simply hold a Bible in my hands.

I have not learnt what I am going to say off by heart. I do have notes which I have worked hard on, but they are at home.

I am not saying that every Bible teacher should preach without notes. And I am certainly not saying that it is somehow more spiritual to preach without notes!

What I am saying is that I think this is the right thing for me at the moment. The day may come, as I get older, that a good friend will tell me that notes would help me to be clearer and crisper in what I say.

But for now I am happy to teach the Bible without using notes.

Most of us will use notes of some kind. What I want to encourage you to do is not to over-use them.

c. Too much "presentation"

As you read this I am over 60 years old, so I may well just be out of date. I think a presentation programme (e.g. PowerPoint) is a great servant but a disastrous master.

If a presentation programme is used too much it distracts the listeners from the word of God. And the danger is that it nudges them into listening-to-a-lecture mode.

But if a presentation programme is used, say, simply to reinforce the structure-with-headings, it can be a huge help.

It is up to you to decide what is too much and what is just right.

3. Keep practising

This means asking God for opportunities to teach the Bible.

But you can also practise when you are reading the Bible in your own time with God. Spend a few minutes looking for a structure-with-headings. Let that become a habit and you will grow in your abilities.

Paul writes this to Timothy – and if you think God has given you the gift of teaching, imagine that he is saying it to you:

"Do your best to present yourself to God as one approved, a worker who does not need to be ashamed and who correctly handles the word of truth." 2 Timothy 2:15

If you are not sure if you have been given the gift of teaching, ask the Holy Spirit to show you as you try to put into practice the things you have been reading about in this book.

And if you think that God has given you this gift, ask the Spirit to confirm this by strengthening the characteristics we looked at on pages 52-56.

But keep practising!

4. Long for a supernatural event

I called this book *How to Teach the Bible so that People Meet God* – and that is an astonishing thing to aim at.

We cannot create an encounter with God. Only the Holy Spirit can do that.

But if what he uses more than anything else to change people's lives is the Bible, Bible teachers have an amazing privilege. As they teach God's word the Holy Spirit may choose to make this a supernatural event.

Doesn't that make you want to pray?

Something to do (13)

1. **Look through the main headings of this Conclusion again.**
   Write down the things that you feel are important for you, and take time to pray about them.

2. **Run through the whole of this book in your mind, thinking especially about the following:**
   A Model
   A Method
   Study the passage in context
   Find a structure-with-headings
   Add the flesh and the blood
   A Mentor
   Write a list of 3, 4 or 5 things you want to do as a result of having worked through this book.
   And pray about them.

The Mark Experiment

How Mark's Gospel can help you know Jesus better

Andrew Page

If you are looking for a new way into Mark's Gospel and you long to allow the Gospel to help you worship and experience Jesus, The Mark Experiment is the book for you.

In The Mark Experiment Andrew Page shows you how to commit the Gospel to memory and explains how learning to meditate on the Gospel events has transformed his relationship with Jesus. Think what this might mean for your understanding of the life and ministry of Jesus.

One exciting result of this book has been the development of an innovative drama in which a team of 15 Christians from a church or student group acts out every incident in the Gospel of Mark as theatre-in-the-round. The Mark Drama is now being performed in many countries around the world.

www.themarkdrama.com

ISBN 978-3-937965-21-5
106 pp. · Pb. · £ 8.00
VTR Publications
info@vtr-online.com
http://www.vtr-online.com

Lightning Source UK Ltd.
Milton Keynes UK
UKHW01f2206191018
330843UK00002B/54/P